Sea Jellies

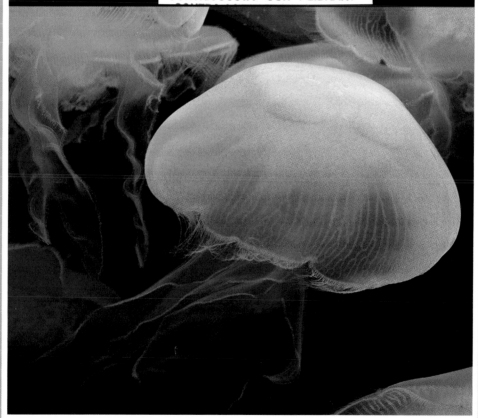

By Mary Logue

THE CHILD'S WORLD®

CHANHASSEN, MINNESOTA

Published in the United States of America by The Child's World®
PO Box 326, Chanhassen, MN 55317-0326
800-599-READ
www.childsworld.com

Content Advisers:
Jim Rising, PhD,
Professor of Zoology,
University of Toronto,
Department of Zoology,
Toronto, Ontario,
Canada, and Trudy
Rising, Educational
Consultant, Toronto,
Ontario, Canada

Photo Credits:
Cover/frontispiece: Sea World Inc./Corbis; cover corner: Mark A. Johnson/Corbis
Interior: Animals Animals/Earth Scenes: 4 (W.A.N.T. Photography), 12 (Carol Geake),
14 (Linden H. Adler), 17 (Marian Bacon), 20 (Boyle & Boyle); Corbis: 6 (Kevin
Schafer), 23 (Neil Miller; Papilio); Dembinsky Photo Associates: 8 (Jesse Cancelmo),
16 (Joe Sroka), 18 (Marilyn Kazmers), 27 (Darrell Gulin), 29 (E. R. Degginger); Digital
Vision/Punchstock: 22; A. Flowers/L. Newman/Photo Researchers: 24; OSF/Animals
Animals/Earth Scenes: 10 (Kathy Atkinson), 19 (D. Fleetham); OSF/F. Ehrenstrom/
Animals Animals/Earth Scenes: 7, 13; OSF/ Peter Parks/Animals Animals/Earth Scenes:
15, 25, 26.

The Child's World®: Mary Berendes, Publishing Director

Editorial Directions, Inc.: E. Russell Primm, Editorial Director; Pam Rosenberg, Line
Editor; Katie Marsico, Assistant Editor; Matt Messbarger, Editorial Assistant; Susan
Hindman, Copy Editor; Susan Ashley, Proofreader; Peter Garnham, Terry Johnson,
Olivia Nellums, Katherine Trickle, and Stephen Carl Wender, Fact Checkers; Tim
Griffin/IndexServ, Indexer; Cian Loughlin O'Day, Photo Researcher; Linda S. Koutris,
Photo Selector

The Design Lab: Kathleen Petelinsek, Design and Page Production

Library of Congress Cataloging-in-Publication Data
Logue, Mary.
  Sea jellies / by Mary Logue.
      p. cm. — (Science around us)
  Includes index.
  ISBN 1-59296-272-6 (library bound : alk. paper) 1. Cnidaria—Juvenile literature.
2. Jellyfishes—Juvenile literature. I. Title. II. Science around us (Child's World (Firm))
  QL375.6.L64 2005
  593.8—dc22   2004003648

TABLE OF CONTENTS

CHAPTER ONE

WHAT IS A SEA JELLY?

I f you are swimming in the ocean and see a nearly **transparent**

animal that looks like a lovely parachute floating by, enjoy

watching it—but take care! That shimmering creature—a jellyfish—

could deliver a nasty sting.

A diver observes a sea jelly near Australia's Great Barrier Reef.

Jellyfish are in the same animal group as sea anemones, corals, and hydroids. This group is called cnidarians (ni-DAR-ee-enz), which means "stinging **nettles**" in Greek. They all have one thing in common: stinging cells that help them capture their food. These stinging cells are located on their **tentacles.**

As a group, these animals are commonly called sea jellies. Much of their bodies is made up of a **gelatinous** substance. Because these creatures come in so many jewel-tone colors—including raspberry red and deep blueberry blue—some of them look like beautiful bits of floating jelly. They might even look good enough to eat—but they're not.

Sea jellies are invertebrates, which means they have no backbones. But they do have nervous systems that run

> Jellyfish have been on the planet for more than 650 million years, drifting through all the oceans. This makes them much older than the dinosaurs.

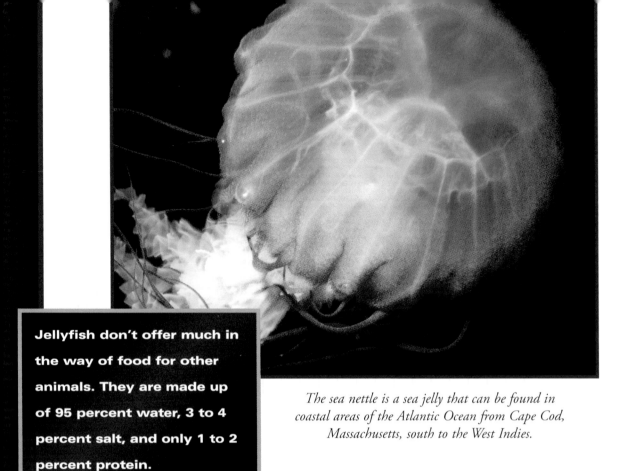

Jellyfish don't offer much in the way of food for other animals. They are made up of 95 percent water, 3 to 4 percent salt, and only 1 to 2 percent protein.

The sea nettle is a sea jelly that can be found in coastal areas of the Atlantic Ocean from Cape Cod, Massachusetts, south to the West Indies.

through their bodies. They also have

mouths and stomachlike cavities to digest food.

Jellies breathe, or pull in oxygen, in a very simple manner: It is

absorbed through their skin. Waste products also leave through the

skin, going back out into the water.

Jellyfish spend their lives anchored to the seafloor or floating

through the ocean currents. By relaxing and contracting their bodies, they are able to move through the water. Their tentacles comb

through the water, gathering food.

There are about 10,000 **species** of cnidarians. Most of them

live in the ocean, but a few can be

found in freshwater lakes.

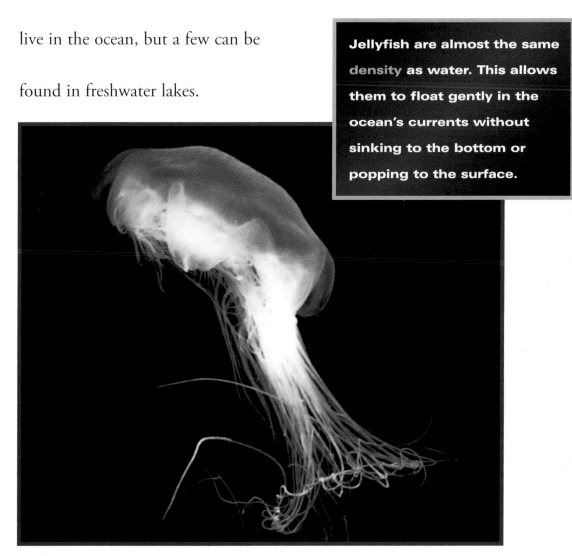

Jellyfish are almost the same density as water. This allows them to float gently in the ocean's currents without sinking to the bottom or popping to the surface.

The sting of the blue lion's mane sea jelly can be fatal to humans. Some fish, however, are not affected by the poison and feed on this sea jelly.

CHAPTER TWO

HOW SEA JELLIES LIVE

Most sea jellies take one of two forms—a **polyp,** attached to the ocean floor like coral, or a **medusa** that floats through the water. Some sea jellies start out as polyps and become medusas.

Some sea jellies are polyps and live their lives attached to the sea floor, such as these soft coral polyps in the Red Sea.

These two forms confused scientists for many years. They

thought the two forms were actually two different kinds of animal.

Many jelly polyps reproduce by making copies of themselves.

The polyp grows a bud on its body. The bud breaks off of the parent

and grows into an exact copy of the original polyp. This process is a

form of **cloning.**

Other sea jellies reproduce sexually—sperm and eggs come

together to create a new creature. Most adult jellyfish are either male

or female. The females release eggs and the males release sperm into

the water. The eggs and sperm come together and grow into small

larvae. Jellyfish larvae are called planula.

The larvae settle on the bottom of the

ocean and grow into polyps.

All jellies are predators. They

The compass jellyfish begins life as a male. As an adult, it is both male and female. It can fertilize its own eggs. Finally, it turns into a female.

capture other sea creatures—fish, shrimp, and plankton—with their

stinging tentacles and eat them.

Whether they are coral or jellyfish, all sea jellies have tentacles.

Some jellyfish have tentacles that are 18 meters (60 feet) long. Many

corals have tentacles that are less than 1 centimeter ($^1/_2$ inch) in

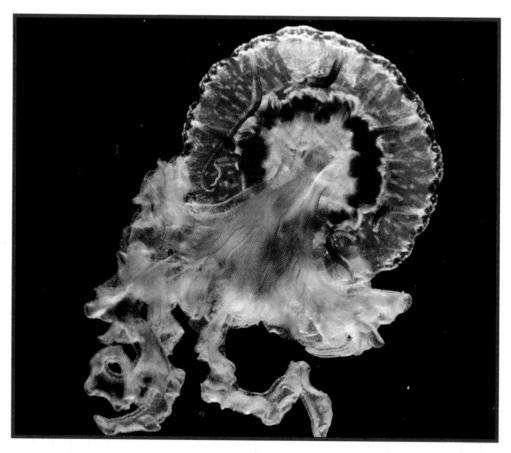

*This purple stinger, like all jellyfish, has tentacles that are covered
with nematocysts, commonly known as stinging cells.*

length. Some sea jellies can have up to 800 tentacles!

Whatever their number or size, these tentacles are covered with stinging cells. Coiled inside each of these cells is a barbed thread. When the tentacle is touched, this thread springs out to sting and entangle the prey. The prey is then pulled into the jelly's mouth and eaten.

The tentacles are also used to defend against predators. But there are a few animals that are not affected by the tentacles' poison. Some sea stars can eat coral. And jellyfish are a favorite food of some sea slugs and sea turtles.

> The teeth of a parrot fish are joined together to form a "beak." They use their beak to break up the hard exterior of coral and get to the soft polyps inside.

All jellies have the ability to **regenerate** their tentacles. When a tentacle is worn away or torn off by an enemy, the jelly grows a new one.

CHAPTER THREE

DIFFERENT KINDS OF JELLYFISH

There are more than 200 different kinds of jellyfish. Some are

smaller than your fingernail and some are larger than you are!

The most common jellyfish is the moon jellyfish. It is found in

every ocean. Not very large, usually only 15 to 25 centimeters (6 to

10 inches) in length, it is transparent. You

A *Desmonema glaciale* jellyfish is so hardy it can live near the ice floes of Antarctica. Its tentacles are often more than 4 meters (13 feet) long.

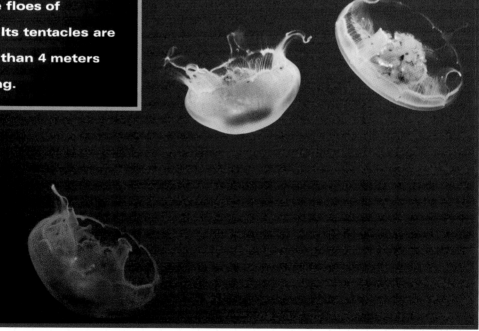

Moon jellies are different from many other sea jellies because they don't have the long tentacles that people usually associate with jellyfish.

A lion's mane sea jelly was the murder weapon in The Adventure of the Lion's Mane, *a Sherlock Holmes mystery.*

can see the insides of this animal, even the food it is digesting.

The lion's mane jellyfish is the largest jellyfish. Its bell (the main body) can be more than 1 meter (3 feet) across, and its tentacles can hang down more than 9 meters (30 feet). The tentacles are very fine and can be hard to see. It was given its name because the tentacles hanging down from its bell are dark brown and look like a ruffled

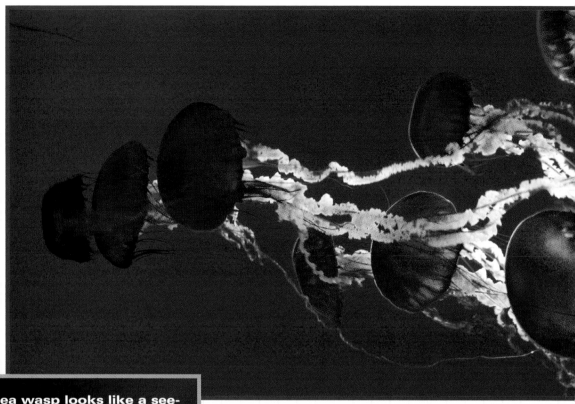

A sea wasp looks like a see-through box that's been decorated with delicate white ribbons. Only 25 centimeters (10 inches) across, it is one of the most poisonous jellyfish. One sting can kill a swimmer in three minutes.

Sea nettles live in water that is part salt water and part freshwater, at the mouths of rivers that empty into the ocean.

lion's mane. It is a common jellyfish in Australia's coastal waters. Its sting is painful, but not deadly.

Another jellyfish, this one commonly found in the waters around the United States, is the sea nettle. It lives in brackish waters—part salt water, part freshwater—at the mouths of rivers that feed into the ocean. Sea nettles are plentiful in the Chesapeake Bay on the Atlantic Ocean. They are a nuisance for swimmers but are good for the oysters. Sea nettles eat the comb jellies that feed on young oysters.

The most dangerous animal found in the waters of Australia's Great Barrier Reef is a tiny jellyfish called the irukandji. This jelly's bell is only about 1 centimeter ($^1/_2$ inch) across, and its tentacles are

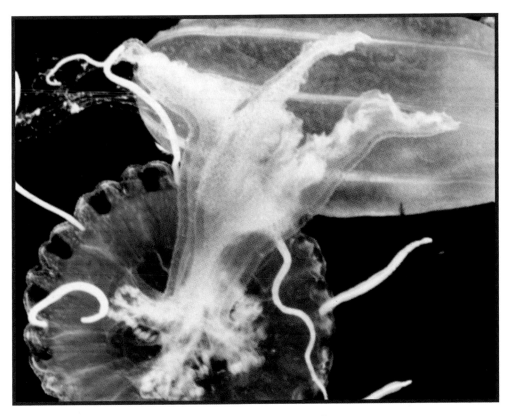

A sea nettle eats a comb jelly.

The beautiful Great Barrier Reef of Australia is home to many sea jellies.

between $2^1/_2$ and 25 centimeters (1 and 10 inches) long. Because it

is colorless and so small, it is difficult to see. The irukandji's sting

can make you very sick and sometimes can even be fatal. Swimming

in this area during the summer months (October through May in

Australia) is not recommended. People who do swim there during

that time often wear protective clothing called stinger suits.

CHAPTER FOUR

FLOWER ANIMALS AND CORAL REEFS

Sea anemones look like upside-down jellyfish. This is not surprising because they are close relatives. They are in the same group of animals as the corals and are sometimes known as flower animals. Though sea anemones look like plants, they are actually meat-eating animals.

Sea anemones live only as polyps secured to the ocean floor. Their tentacles stretch out from around their mouths at the tips of their tubelike bodies. Because sea anemones don't move, they must wait for their food to

The magnificent anemone is a colorful animal.

The brooding anemone is one kind of anemone that sometimes provides protection for hermit crabs.

swim by. Then they reach out with their tentacles, sting their prey, and push it into their mouths.

These fantastic sea creatures come in many different colors, shapes, and sizes. They can be green, orange, or purple—even red with white polka dots. With their brightly colored tentacles circling the top of the tube, they certainly do look like flowers. There are more than 1,000 different species of sea anemones. Most of them are found in shallow waters by seacoasts.

Sea anemones reproduce by dividing, or cloning, themselves. A new sea anemone sprouts out from the side of the parent animal. Some of them also reproduce by releasing eggs and sperm.

Clown fish often stay near sea anemones. They aren't bothered by the anemones' sting and are protected by the anemones' tentacles. In return, the clown fish clean the sea anemones' tentacles, eating any leftover food bits.

Clownfish and sea anemones often have a mutually beneficial relationship.

The coast of Oregon at low tide, a dangerous time for sea anemones.

Low tide is a danger to animals, such as sea anemones, that live

attached to the ocean floor near shore. When the ocean level drops,

the anemones are no longer in the water. They pull into a small ball

to stay moist. If they are exposed to air and light for too long, they

will die.

The giant sea anemone can grow to be up to 25 centimeters (10 inches) in diameter. Some kinds of shrimp and other sea creatures live in the protection of its tentacles, while avoiding being stung themselves.

Sea anemones have very few animal

enemies. One sea creature that does eat

them is the grey sea slug.

Have you ever wondered where

reefs in the ocean come from? Would you believe many of them

were formed by small sea creatures called coral? It's true. Coral

polyps are similar to anemones, but they form hard shells to live in.

When thousands of these make homes next to one another, a solid

mass is created. These masses are known as coral reefs.

Coral reefs provide food and shelter for many fish and other sea animals. They also help protect seacoasts from erosion.

The Great Barrier Reef of Australia is the largest coral reef in the world. It is almost the size of the state of California. Parts of it rise up nearly 180 meters (600 feet) from the ocean floor.

A coral reef is a large community of sea animals living together—much like a city. Coral reefs provide a protective home for many sea creatures. Coral can live and grow only when the ocean water is very clear. They need light to grow. As the ocean waters become polluted, these reefs are threatened.

CHAPTER FIVE

HYDROIDS AND COMB JELLIES

Hydroids are the simplest form of jellies. One common species is the hydra, which measures only about 1 centimeter ($^1/_2$ inch) long and lives in freshwater ponds. If you saw one, you might think it was a piece of white yarn float-

ing in the water. But under

a microscope, you would

see that it has deli-

cate tentacles.

Other hydroids take

both the polyp and the

medusa forms. The polyps

often live in colonies. One

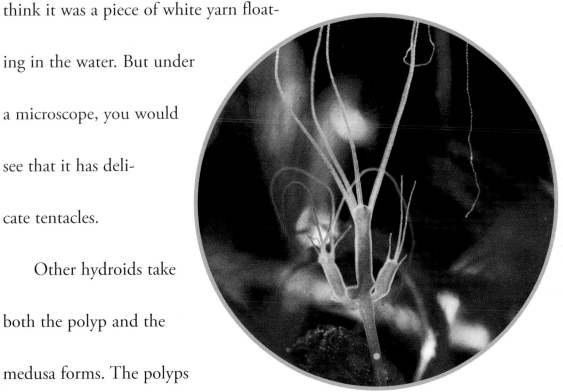

The brown hydra is found in freshwater in the northern hemisphere and parts of Australia.

example of a hydroid that lives in colonies is the Portuguese man-of-war. This animal may look like a large, floating jellyfish, but it's actually a whole small community of polyps. A colony is composed of about 1,000 animals that work together. Some members catch the food, others

If you cut a hydra in two, both pieces will regenerate and you will soon have two hydras. They move by using their tentacles to somersault through the water.

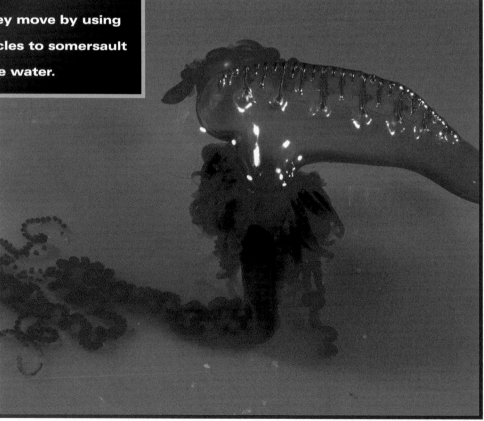

The Portuguese man-of-war is sometimes called the blue bottle, because of the appearance of its blue body, or "float."

A close-up view of the tentacles of a Portuguese man-of-war shows its many stinging cells.

digest it, and still others produce new animals. A huge blue or pur-

ple gas-filled "float" allows the colony to stay on the surface of the

ocean and be blown around by the sea winds. The polyps' long ten-

tacles can reach a length of up to 50 meters (165 feet).

Comb jellies, while similar to jellyfish, are in a separate group of

animals. The "combs" are bands of hairlike structures called cilia that

are used for swimming. These animals don't have stinging cells.

Comb jellies can be found throughout the world.

Tide pools are great places to observe sea anemones and other marine creatures.

Instead they use sticky cells called colloblasts to catch their prey.

There are many different kinds of sea jellies in Earth's oceans.

Tide pools and coral reefs are great places to observe them. So next

time you are near the ocean, ask an adult to join you in exploring

the coast. You may be lucky enough to see some of these simple,

beautiful animals.

GLOSSARY

cloning (KLOHN-ing) Cloning is a process in which a new living thing is formed from the cells of the parent so that the offspring is an exact copy of its parent.

density (DEN-si-tee) Density is a measure of how light or heavy something is for its size. To find the density of an object, you divide its mass by its volume.

gelatinous (jeh-LAT-tuh-nus) Something that is gelatinous has to do with gelatin, a clear substance obtained from bones and other tissues from animals. Gelatin is used to make desserts and jellies.

medusa (meh-DOO-suh) A medusa is the adult form of a jellyfish.

nettles (NET-uhls) Nettles are plants with sharp hairs that sting if you touch them.

polyp (POL-ip) A polyp is a small invertebrate animal with a tubelike body and a mouth surrounded by tentacles.

regenerate (ree-JEN-uh-rayt) To regenerate means to grow again.

species (SPEE-sheez) A species is a certain type of living thing. Sea jellies of the same species can mate and produce young. Sea jellies of different species cannot produce young together.

tentacles (TEN-tuh-kuhlz) Tentacles are the long, bendable limbs of animals such as jellyfish and sea anemones.

transparent (trans-PAIR-unt) Something that is transparent lets light through so that objects on the other side of it can be seen.

▸ A group of sea jellies is called a smack.

▸ A sea pen colony is made up of many polyps attached to a main trunk. This sea anemone looks like an old-fashioned quill pen.

▸ Brain coral is one of the most interesting coral species. It looks like a giant brain. A colony of brain coral might weigh more than a ton and grow to more than 1 meter (3 feet) across.

▸ The jellyfish's scientific name (coe-lenterates) means "cup animals." Its bell looks like a cup turned upside down, floating in the water.

▸ A jellyfish or a plastic bag? From a distance, it is hard for some ani-mals to tell the difference between a plastic bag floating on the water or a sea jelly. Sea turtles and birds have been known to eat plastic bags, with deadly results.

▸ The sea turtle is one of the few predators of the Portuguese man-of-war.

Sea pens give off a bright greenish light if they are touched.

THE ANIMAL KINGDOM

VERTEBRATES

fish

amphibians

reptiles

birds

mammals

INVERTEBRATES

sponges

worms

insects

spiders & scorpions

mollusks & crustaceans

sea stars

sea jellies

HOW TO LEARN MORE ABOUT SEA JELLIES

At the Library
Green, Jen. *A Coral Reef.*
New York: Crabtree Publishing, 2002.

Landau, Elaine. *Jellyfish.*
Danbury, Conn.: Children's Press, 1999.

Sharth, Sharon. *Jellyfish.*
Chanhassen, Minn.: The Child's World, 2001.

Sharth, Sharon. *Sea Jellies: From Corals to Jellyfish.*
Danbury, Conn.: Franklin Watts, 2002.

On the Web
VISIT OUR HOME PAGE FOR LOTS OF LINKS ABOUT SEA JELLIES:
http://www.childsworld.com/links.html
Note to Parents, Teachers, and Librarians: We routinely check our Web links to make sure they're safe, active sites—so encourage your readers to check them out!

Places to Visit or Contact
AUDUBON AQUARIUM OF THE AMERICAS
To see the world's largest exhibit of sea jellies
1 Canal Street
New Orleans, LA 70130
800/744-7394

JOHN G. SHEDD AQUARIUM
To see the Wild Reef exhibit
1200 South Lake Shore Drive
Chicago, IL 60605
312/939-2435

INDEX

About the Author

Award-winning poet and mystery writer **Mary Logue** was born and raised in Minnesota. She has written and translated many books for children, including *Dancing with an Alien.*